The Plane

Sumehra Addnan

Archway Publishing books may be ordered through booksellers or by contacting:

Archway Publishing
1663 Liberty Drive
Bloomington, IN 47403
www.archwaypublishing.com
844-669-3957

Because of the dynamic nature of the Internet, any web addresses or links contained in this
book may have changed since publication and may no longer be valid. The views expressed
in this work are solely those of the author and do not necessarily reflect the views of
the publisher, and the publisher hereby disclaims any responsibility for them.

Interior Image Credit: Illustrator & Sumehra Addnan

ISBN: 978-1-6657-0972-9 (sc)
ISBN: 978-1-6657-0970-5 (hc)
ISBN: 978-1-6657-0971-2 (e)

Print information available on the last page.

Archway Publishing rev. date: 10/04/2021

ARCHWAY
PUBLISHING

I dedicated this book
to my parents and my
pet fish "Goldie"

One sunny fine windy day
in the Spring, flowers were
blossoming in the park, and
the trees were filled with
different types of fruits.

Three friends, Jay, Darryl,
and Rose arrived at the park.

Each of them brought their own entertainment, Darryl brought a soccer ball, Rose had a weaved basket for collecting flowers, and Jay brought his paper plane.

As Jay was playing with the plane, Darryl warned him that his toy could hurt someone because it had a sharp nose and was flying fast.

Jay, however, ignored Darryl's advice, and continued throwing his paper plane around.

While everybody was busy
playing, suddenly the
plane flew around and hit
Darryl in the left eye.

Darryl started crying; and Rose and Jay immediately came to his aid. "Are you okay?" Jay asked. "It hurts a little." Darryl replied.

They informed their parents about what happened to Darryl, and later on Darryl's parents took him to the hospital.

When Darryl came back to the
park the next day, he could
be seen wearing an eye-patch,
which the doctors gave him.

Jay felt bad for hurting
his friend, so he apologized
to Darryl and Darryl
accepted his apology.

They continued being
the best of friends.

Jay learned an important
lesson from this experience
and now he makes sure that he
never plays with sharp objects.

Printed in the United States
by Baker & Taylor Publisher Services